WIRTSCHAFTSDEUTSCH

FÜR ANFÄNGER

WIRTSCHAFTSDEUTSCH

FÜR ANFÄNGER

Shannon Keenan Greene

Christopher Newport University

Neuss Publishing

Neuss Publishing

Cover Image by Luigi Mengato

© 2014, Neuss Publishing

Image p. 3 © Luigi Mengato
Image p. 9 by MOCCU
Image p. 19 by of Wolfgang Lonlen
Image p. 25 by Felix Montino Image p.
39 by Sven-Christian Kindler Image p.
57 by Gerhard Glebener Image p. 71 by
Alex
Image p. 91 by Kokorowashinjin Image
p. 117 by Neo 11
Images by Flickr Creative Commons:
pp. 3, 9,19,25,39, 57,71,91,117, cover

ISBN 978-1-942203-13-1

Table of Contents

Kapitel 1

Woher kommen Sie?

- Basic Introductions
- Simple verb endings
- Gender of nouns
- Numbers 1-20
- Description with simple adjectives
- Formal and informal
- German business etiquette

Dialog

Ich heiße Markus Schneider.
Es freut mich.
Wie heißen Sie?
Jonas. Jonas Kuhn.

ich heiße – I am called, my name is...
Wie heißen Sie? – What's your name?
Es freut mich – Nice to meet you.

> For the pronunciation of any word, go to www.leo.org and click on the sound icon to hear an audiofile.

A letter like a capital „ß" in the middle of the word, also looks like „ß" or „β", is a double „s" and is pronounced like „s"

Dialog

Woher kommen Sie?
Ich komme aus Bonn. Und Sie?
Ich komme aus Stuttgart.
Es freut mich.
Es freut mich auch.

woher – from where?
Woher kommen Sie? – Where do you come from?
Ich komme aus ... – I come from ...
auch – also

Dialog

Wie geht es Ihnen?
Es geht mir gut. Und Ihnen?
Es geht mir auch gut, danke.
Gut.

Wie geht's? = Wie geht es
Wie geht es Ihnen?- How's it going for you?, How are you?
Ihnen – for you
mir-for me
Es geht mir gut. – I'm well, thank you. (Literally: It goes well for me")

Give the German phrase:

1. good, well
2. for me (one word)
3. for you
4. you (begins with capital S)
5. how

Give the German phrase:

1. What's your name?
2. How are you?
3. Where do you come from?
4. My name is...
5. I come from...
6. I'm well, thank you. And you?
7. It's nice to meet you.

German verbs conjugate: that means there is a different ending depending on the subject of the verb.

Ich komm<u>e</u> aus Bremen.
Sie komm<u>en</u> aus Hannover.

ich –I	wir-we
du – you (informal)	ihr – you (plural, informal)
er – he sie-she	sie – they Sie – you (formal)

Please note that „sie" means she or they. Only the verb ending will tell you whether it is she or they:

sie relax<u>t</u> – she relaxes
sie relax<u>en</u> – they relax

„Sie" (always capitalized) means you.

It can get confusing with sie, sie, and Sie.

Give the German word:

1. she
2. they
3. you (formal)
4. you (informal, begins with d...)
5. he
6. it – es
7. I – ich

which sie is it?
she-they-you

1. sie wohnt in Bremen
2. sie wohnen in Bremen
3. Sie sprechen ein bisschen Deutsch
4. sie sagt „hallo"
5. Sie haben einen Dell-Computer
6. sie sprechen gut Englisch

Dialog

Woher kommen Sie?
Ich komme aus Frankfurt.
Und wo wohnen Sie jetzt?
Ich wohne in Regensburg.

wo- where?
woher-from where?
und- and
Wo wohnen Sie jetzt? – Where do you live now?

Note:
Ich komme aus ...
but
Ich wohne in ...

ich wohne	wir wohnen
du wohnst	ihr wohnt
er,sie,es wohnt	sie wohnen Sie wohnen

ich komme	wir kommen
du kommst	ihr kommt
er,sie,es kommt	sie kommen Sie kommen

Translate:

1. They live in Bamberg.
2. You (du) come from Essen
3. I live in Bonn.
4. I come from ... [your city or town]
5. She lives in Augsburg.
6. Niklas lives in Köln.
7. Tim and Katja come from Jena.

Verb conjugation

ich	-e	wir	-en
du	-st	ihr	-t
er,sie,es	-t	sie	-en
		Sie	-en

There are three genders for nouns in German:

der Partner (masculine)
die Teambildung (feminine)
das Geschäft (neuter)

The word „the" is: der, die or das

What gender is each word?
1. die Arbeit
2. der Chef
3. der Kollege
4. das Team
5. die Besprechung

At dict.leo.org („leo"), look up the meaning of each word:
1. die Arbeit
2. der Chef
3. der Kollege
4. das Team
5. die Besprechung

Also at leo.org, look up 10 useful words for your business. For each noun, include der, die or das.

The word „a" („/"an")
ein means a(n) for masculine and neuter nouns
eine means a(n) for feminine nouns
If you see the word „eine Tafel" it must be feminine.
If you see the word „ein Stuhl" it might me masculine or neuter; you can't tell from „ein" (it's masculine)

Convert „the" to „a(n)":

1. die Arbeit – eine Arbeit
2. der Chef
3. der Kollege
4. das Team
5. die Besprechung

Numbers 1-20

1.   eins
2.   zwei
3.   drei
4.   vier
5.   fünf
6.   sechs
7.   sieben
8.   acht
9.   neun
10. zehn
11. elf
12. zwölf
13. drei-zehn (hyphenation for teaching purposes only)
14. vier-zehn
15. fünf-zehn
16. sech-zehn (-s- drops out)
17. sieb-zehn (-en- drops out)
18. acht-zehn
19. neun-zehn
20. zwanzig

Denken Sie außerhalb der Box!

(Think outside the box.)

Use leo.org to find the meaning of each adjective below:

1) sportlich
2) fleiBig
3) organisiert
4) lustig
5) freundlich
6) extrovertiert
7) sozial

Descriptions: Ich bin..., er ist..., sie ist...

ich bin – I am
er ist – he is
sie ist – she is
Sie sind – you are

Ich bin fleiBig — I am hard-working.
Kristin ist auch fleiBig.
Max ist philosophisch.

Describe your self, saying Ich bin... or Ich bin nicht (I am not)...

sportlich
fleiBig
organisiert
lustig
freundlich
extrovertiert
sozial

For each person below, choose an adjective above, and use the verb „ist"

1. Charlotte — Charlotte ist extrovertiert
2. Harald
3. Pia
4. Thomas
5. Danuta

the verb „to be" is irregular:

ich bin	wir sind
du bist	ihr seid
er/sie/es ist	sie sind, Sie sind

Formal and informal

Wie geht's **Ihnen**? – How are you? (formal you)
Wie geht's **dir**? – How are you? (informal you)

Most offices use Sie, but each company has its own culture. In formal speeach, Sie means you and Ihnen means „to you" or „for you"

Wie geht es <u>Ihnen</u>? – literally: How goes it <u>for you</u>?

Dialog

Servus, Max.
Moin moin, Joachim.
Ach ja, Sie kommen aus Norddeutschland.
Und Sie kommen aus Bayern!
Geht's Ihnen gut?
Ja, mir geht es gut, danke.

servus – hello (used in Bavaria and Austria)
moin moin – hello (used in Northern Germany)
Bayern – Bavaria

Kultur

Shake hands when you meet for the first time and often, each time you greet someone beyond just passing by and saying hello. If there is a difference in rank, usually the more important person offers his/her hand and then the other person shakes. Stand close for a handshake, and expect one strong shake (not three, as in many other business cultures).

Use the formal word for you, "Sie," unless someone tells you to use "du." German colleagues often use first names and "Sie."

German workplaces are for work and not chit-chat, surfing the internet, or personal calls.

Kapitel 2

Ich arbeite gern

- What do you like?
- ich mag and gern
- Nominative versus Accusative
- Verb infinitives
- Ich kann and ich werde (I can and I will!)
- German notions regarding work and careers.

What do you like?

Ich mag den Porsche 911 (neun-hundert-elf)
Ich mag Nutella auf Brot. (auf Brot=on bread)

Was mögen Sie? – What do you like?
Ich mag...

Choose from the list below and say Ich mag or Ich mag....nicht. Please note that „nicht" comes <u>after</u> the direct object.

1. den Chef (the boss)
2. Microsoft Office
3. Schokolade
4. neue Trends im Computing (neu=new)
5. dunkles Bier (dunkel=dark)
6. Gleitzeit (flextime, working flexible hours)
7. das Online-Lernen

Ich mag.. is used with nouns: „I like dark beer." (Beer is a noun). Notice that 1-7 above are all nouns.

For verbs, it's more complicated:

Ich singe **gern** – I like to sing
Ich schwimme gern – I like to swim
Ich surfe gern im Internet.
Ich spiele gern Videospiele. (spielen= to play)
Hans spricht gern Deutsch. (Hans likes to speak German)

sprechen is an irregular verb:
Ich spreche Deutsch
but
Hans <u>spricht</u> Deutsch

Answer in full sentences:
1) Spielen Sie gern Videospiele?
2) Surfen Sie gern im Internet?
3) Spielen Sie gern Fußball?
4) Arbeiten Sie gern mit PowerPoint?
(arbeiten=to work; mit=with)

Sie mögen alles! – Say that you like everything.
Say „Ich mag..." or „Ich ... gern," as appropriate.

Ich mag – for nouns
Ich ... gern – for verbs

1) spiele ... Tischtennis
2) die FC Bayern Fußball-Mannschaft
3) Kaffee mit Zucker (with sugar)
4) laufe (I run)
5) helles Bier (lager bier)
6) wohne ... in Hamburg
7) Deutschland
8) singe
9) komme . .. nach Deutschland
10) Österreich und die Schweiz (Austria and Switzerland)

A verb has a subject and often, a direct object.

I like Switzerland.
I have a laptop.

In German, there is a concept called case. Every noun phrase has a „case."

If a noun phrase is a subject then it is „in the subject case." If it's the direct object (like Switzerland or a laptop, above) then it is „in the direct object case.")

All subjects are in the NOMINATIVE CASE (the subject case)
All direct objects are in the ACCUSATIVE CASE (the direct object case).

Nominative (subject)
Accusative (direct object)

Find the nominatives and accusatives below:

1. I like Switzerland.
2. I have a laptop.
3. Mein sister runs a small company.
4. My partner and I purchased stock in her company.*

*the direct object is just „stock"; *„in her company"* is a prepositional phrase: it's not a subject or a direct object

Masculine nouns as direct objects:

<u>Der</u> Mann ist mein Geschäftspartner. (business partner)
Ich kenne <u>den</u> Mann.

When a masculine noun is in the direct object case (the accusative case), it will be „den Mann" instead of „der Mann" or „den Fußball" instead of „der Fußball."

<u>der</u> Mann – the subject of the sentence
<u>den</u> Mann – the direct object of the sentence

Let's talk about a soccer ball.

Use „<u>der</u> FuBball" or „<u>den</u> FuBball" for each blank.

1._____ ist neu. (neu=new)

2.Ich mag _____. Er ist aus Leder. (Leder=leather)

3.Haben Sie _____?

4._____ist schmutzig. (dirty, soiled)

For 1-4 above, it was necessary to decide: is „soccer ball" the subject of the verb or is it the direct object?

Ich mag... :

Say you like these things. If it is a masculine noun, change der to den.

1) der Porsche 911
2) die neue Idee von Max (Max's new idea; von=of,from)
3) das Haus an der Ecke (the house on the corner)
4) der Geschäftsplan (business plan)

That is the concept of case, in its most basic form. Remember, case refers to noun phrases, not verbs.

Back to verbs

Verbs almost always end in –en. The infinitive of the verb is the basic form, ending in –en. If you take away the –en, then you have the Stem of a verb.

Question: to conjugate a verb (see chapter 1), do you add the conjugation endings to the Infinitive or the Stem?

There are some uses for the <u>infinitive</u> of a verb.

Ich kann sehen – I can see

After „ich kann," use the infinitive of the verb:

Ich kann die Arbeit <u>machen</u>. – I can do the work.

Ich kann mit Ihnen ein Bier <u>trinken</u>. (mit Ihnen=with you)

Say what you can do

Ich kann ...

1)   die Arbeit mit Katja machen.
2)   den Plan mit Harald diskutieren.
3)   mit Uwe einen Kaffee trinken und die
Arbeit diskutieren.

The future tense.
Ich werde plus the Infinitive of the verb
creates the future tense
(I will..., I'm going to...)

Ich werde nach Deutschland fliegen. – I will
fly to Germany.

**Take your three sentences from the exercise
above and change „ich kann" to „ich
werde" (I will).**

1.
2.
3.

Kultur

In Germany, work is an important part of the culture and having a profession is an important part of one's identity.

At the age of about 9, German school children, in consultation with their parents and their teacher, choose a school that will lead to a profession or a distinctive cluster of professions. These decisions are not made lightly. Of course children can later decide to change to a different school, but this choice is significant in beginning to prepare for a profession. As teenagers, many pupils will begin internships in their chosen occupations while continuing to attend school part-time.

This unique system of apprenticeship derives from feudal Germany.

Coming soon from Kuhn Publishing...

GERMAN CONVERSATION
WITH A
BUSINESS FOCUS
INTERMEDIATE / ADVANCED

Geschäftsdeutsch für Konversationsfähigkeit im Deutschunterricht und für Konversationen mit deutschen Geschäftspartnern

Kapitel 3
Teamarbeit

- Office and email vocabulary
- Setting up an appointment, canceling, postponing
- Prepositions
- The individual and the team in German culture

Using leo.com as needed, fill out the matching column below.

1) das Büro   a. the meeting
2) das Projekt   b. finished
3) der Chef   c. participate
4) der Kollege   d. the project
5) die Arbeit   e. work together
6) die Besprechung   f. the office
7) die Zeitverplanung   g. the planning of
8) fertig   time
9) mitmachen   h. the boss
10)   zusammen   i. the co-worker
   arbeiten   j. the work

Ich werde eine Besprechung vereinbaren. – I am going to arrange a meeting.

Give the German word:
1)   work
2)   participate
3)   together
4)   arrange
5)   office

Dialog

Das Projekt ist sehr kompliziert. (very complicated). Ich werde eine Besprechung vereinbaren.
Ich kann am Donnerstag (on Thursday) kommen.
Geht das? (Does that work?)
Ja, das geht.

Dialog

Können Sie am Donnerstag kommen, Frau Hirsch?
Ja, haben wir eine Besprechung?
Noch nicht aber ich werde etwas vereinbaren.

Können Sie- can you
noch nicht — not yet
etwas — something

Give the German word:
1)   with
2)   of, from
3)   very
4)   also
5)   together
6)   on Thursday
7)   arrange a meeting

Matching column

1)	ich möchte	a.	to say
2)	die Besprechung	b.	at 8 o'clock
3)	Können Sie?	c.	but
4)	der Termin	d.	I would like to
5)	aber	e.	I'll tell him
6)	sprechen	f.	Can you
7)	morgen	g.	the meeting
8)	sagen	h.	speak
9)	um acht Uhr	i.	tomorrow
10)	ich sage ihm Bescheid	j.	the appointment

Dialog

Ich möchte mit Herrn Huber sprechen.
Haben Sie einen Termin?
Nein. Ich möchte einen Termin machen.
Herr Huber hat morgen frei.
Ja gut. Morgen um elf Uhr?
Gut. Ich sage ihm Bescheid.

Ich mache das – can mean „I am doing that (right now) OR „I will do that" (implied future tense)

Dialog

Ist Frau Lehmann im Büro?
Nein, heute nicht.
Ich möchte einen Termin mit ihr machen.
Wie wäre es mit Freitag um vierzehn Uhr?
Ja, das geht. Vielen Dank.

heute nicht-not today
mit ihr — with her
Wie wäre es mit... — How would it be..
mit ihm — with him

Dialog

Rainer, darf ich kurz mit Ihnen sprechen?
Das geht leider nicht. Ich habe keine Zeit.
Morgen also.
Ja, morgen. Wir trinken einen Kaffee zusammen.

kurz- brief, briefly
mit Ihnen — with you
leider — unfortunately
keine Zeit — no time

Give the German word or phrase:

1. appointment
2. with him / her / you
3. at 8 o'clock
4. speak
5. arrange
6. I would like to
7. I don't have any time ("I have no time")

Dialog

Lukas, was machen Sie? Wir haben eine
Besprechung!
Ich sehe nichts in meinem Kalendar.
Ich bin sicher. Wir haben eine Besprechung. Der
Chef ist schon da.
Gut, ich komme sofort.

ich sehe nichts – I see nothing, I don't see
anything
sicher – certain, secure
ich komme sofort – I'm coming right away

Dialog

Frau Meier, guten Tag. Ich habe einen Termin
mit Frau Kuhn.
Nein, Sie haben keinen Termin.
Kann das sein? Es ist Dienstag um vierzehn Uhr,
oder?
Ich sehe nichts. Aber manchmal habe ich
Probleme mit der Software.
Ich bin sicher. Ich habe einen Termin.
Gut. Gehen Sie ruhig hinein.

Gehen Sie ruhig hinein – Go ahead and go in

Dialog

Frau Meier, guten Tag.
Guten Tag, kann ich Ihnen helfen?
Ja, ich habe einen Termin mit Frau Kuhn.
Und wer sind Sie?
Ich heiße Tobias Schneider.
Der Kalendar ist leer. Es tut mir leid. Diese neue
Kalendar-Software is problematisch. Moment
mal, ich werde Frau Kuhn anrufen.

Kann ich Ihnen helfen – Can I help you?
wer-who

Ich werde sie anrufen – I will call her

leer – empty

Es tut mir leid – I'm sorry

dieser, diese, dieses – this

Dialog

Kommt Jonas zu der Besprechung?

Nein, er kommt niemals.

Wieso nicht? Er ist doch in der Arbeitsgruppe.

Ja, aber er ist auch der Chef.

Kommt Annaliese?

Nein, Annaliese ist in Frankfurt.

Und Niklas.

Niklas ist heute krank.

Wer kommt denn?

Sie und ich.

zu – to

niemals – never

wieso nicht? Warum nicht? – why not?

krank –ill

wer – who

doch, denn

 are flavoring words that do not actually mean
anything and cannot be translated into English
doch means something like „indeed" and „denn"
expresses curiosity when asking a question

Give the German word:

1. never
2. ill
3. empty
4. I'm sorry
5. I will call her
6. certain, secure
7. right away
8. Why not? (2 variations)
9. unfortunately
10. I have no time
11. to say
12. at 8 o'clock
13. but
14. I would like to
15. I'll tell him
16. I can, you can
17. the meeting
18. speak
19. tomorrow
20. appointment
21. with him
22. wit her
23. with you
24. at 8 o'clock
25. speak
26. arrange
27. I would like to
28. briefly
29. participate
30. together
31. arrange
32. office
33. the meeting
34. finished
35. the project
36. work together
37. the co-worker
38. the office
39. the planning of time
40. the boss

Prepositions

Can you name 15 prepositions in English?
(in, after, through...)

Here are some prepositions in German:

in-in
für-for
zu-to
mit-with
auf-on top of
unter-under
zwischen-between

After the word „mit," the next word will generally be a word that ends in —m or —r. Can you find 3 examples of this from this chapter so far? (an exception is: mit Ihnen-with you)

1.
2.
3.

Matching column

1. zwischen uns	a. in the city
2. für mich	b. to
3. für Sie	c. with this software
4. in dem Handbuch	d. for me
5. in der Stadt	e. between us
6. zu	f. in the handbook
7. mit dieser Software	g. for you

After a preposition, the noun phrase that follows will be in a case. It may the accusative case, or it may not be. You have to find out if that preposition takes the accusative.

After the word **für** the noun phrase that follows will be accusative.

Das Geschenk (the gift) ist **für** <u>den</u> Chef.

Which word ending looks accusative? What is making it accusative? It is not a direct object, so what other reason could there be for it to be accusative?

Remember, only some prepositions take the accusative, and this is an arbitrary assignment. You have to memorize: für takes the accusative, so any word that follows, if it is masculine accusative, will be den Mann or den Fußball or den Chef (rather than the usual, nominative der).

Here is a chart of endings so far:

	masculine	feminine	neuter	plural
Nominative	der	die	das	die
Accusative	<u>den</u>	die	das	die

The plural endings above are new. We haven't learned those until now. However, do the other endings make sense to you?

Plural nouns have the same definite article („die" meaning „the") regardless of their gender. There is not a different masculine plural, feminine plural, etc.: there's just: plural.

Dialog

Ich haben einen Termin mit Herrn Frank.
Morgen um...neun Uhr. Ja, alles in Ordnung.
Ich muss den Termin leider stornieren (cancel).
Sie werden den Termin nicht einhalten?
Nein, ich kann nicht.
Ich werde den Termin löschen. [Pause] Er ist gelöscht.
Vielen Dank.
Bitte sehr. Und danke, dass Sie mir Bescheid sagen.

alles in Ordnung – everything's in order
leider – unfortunately
einen Termin einhalten – keep an appointment
dass Sie mir Bescheid sagen – that you are telling me
löschen – to delete

Dialog

Kann ich Ihnen helfen?
Ich muss einen Termin absagen.
Mit wem?
Mit Frau Bauer.
Und wie heißen Sie?
Liese Kaufmann.
Sehr gut. Ich habe den Termin gelöscht.

mit wem — with whom
gelöscht — deleted

eine Email

Herr Kohl,

vielen Dank für Ihre Hilfe bisher. (bisher=up until now)

Ich habe noch ein paar technische Fragen über Ihre Arbeit. Auf Seite zwei sprechen Sie über eine Graphik. (a diagram) aber ich sehe keine Graphik. Wäre es möglich (would it be possible), mir (to me) die Graphik per Email zu schicken? (schicken=to send) Ich möchte sie vor unserer Besprechung (before our meeting) genau anschauen. (look at it carefully)

Ich habe ein Treffen mit Herrn Ziegler am Freitag und ich arbeite schon jetzt mit Gerhardt zusammen.

Vielen Dank im Voraus. (in advance)

Mit freundlichen Grüssen,

Max

Kultur

As is well known, German culture emphasizes both the strong individual working alone and also the strength of the team. In teamwork, Germans routinely play a more participatory role and do whatever is helpful or productive for the common goals of the team members. Acknowledging the greater needs of the team and giving up some individual assertion is considered culturally normal. The team is most important and individuals need to accommodate a smooth-running team, not the other way around.

Because of this sense of team achievement without individual superstars, Germans are not always comfortable with the notion of leaders and leadership in the context of teamwork. Often the phrase "primus unter pares," someone chosen to be first among equals, is a preferable way of phrasing and giving shape to the notion of leadership.

Kapitel 4
Zeit ist Geld

- Time expressions: I'm late, I'm on time. How long have you worked here?
- mit and seit + the dative case
- Days of the week, months.
- Gradations of German friendship

German Case

In this chapter we will see a new case called the dative. For now, only one of the new boxes has been filled in.

	masculine	feminine	neuter	plural
Nominative	der	die	das	die
Accusative	den	die	das	die
Dative	dem			

Dialog

Darf ich kurz mit Ihnen sprechen?
Sie haben fünf Minuten. Ich habe einen Termin um sechzehn Uhr.
Es geht um das Projekt. Ich werde es nicht fertig haben.
Können Sie mit Max zusammen arbeiten?
Ja aber Max hat das Software-Projekt.
Dies ist wichtiger. Arbeiten Sie zusammen mit ihm.

darf ich? – may I?
es geht um – It has to do with
fertig haben – have it finished
dies – this
wichtig- important; wichtig*er* – *more* important

Dialog

Wann ist unser Treffen? (das Treffen=die Besprechung)
Nächste Woche. Am Mittwoch.
Wir machen die Arbeit seit einem Jahr und sie ist immer noch nicht fertig (still not finished).
Es gibt viele Details. Rom wurde nicht in einem Tag gebaut.

das Treffen – meeting
seit einem Jahr – since a year, for over a year now
nächste Woche – next week; nächsten Monat – next month
Es gibt – there is or there are
wurde gebaut – was built
ein Tag – a day

Days of the week:

Der Termin ist am Montag.
am Dienstag
am Mittwoch
am Donnerstag
am Freitag
am Samstag
am Sonntag

space and time...
vor means before, nach means after

in spacial contexts though, vor means in front of
and nach means toward

Matching column

1)	um halb 10	a)	at 2 pm
2)	nächste Woche	b)	yesterday
3)	letzte Woche	c)	at 9.30
4)	gestern	d)	before the meeting
5)	am Samstag	e)	next week
6)	übermorgen	f)	after the appointment
7)	vorgestern	g)	the day after tomorrow
8)	um vierzehn Uhr		
9)	nach dem Termin	h)	last week
10)	vor der Besprechung	i)	the day before yesterday
		j)	on Saturday

Dialog

Guten Tag, Herr Hahnemann.
Sie kennen mich seit zehn Jahren.
Und?
Mein Name ist Michael. Sie haben bei uns
Weihnachten gefeiert und Sie nennen mich
Hahnemann.
Also, Michael.
So ist es besser.

seit einem Jahr — for the past year, literally
"since one year"
seit zehn Jahren — for the past ten years, "since
10 years"
bei uns — at my family's house
Weihnachten feiern — celebrate Christmas

62

After some prepositions such as **für**,
the following noun phrase is accusative.

für den Mann, für die Frau, für den Hund (the dog), für das Büro, für den Computer, für die Chefin (female boss)

-in makes nouns feminine:
Chefin – female boss
Studentin – female student

Add the correct form of the definite article (der/die/das/den /etc.):

1.für _____ Chef
2.für ___ Computer
3.für _____ Besprechung
4.für _____ Termin
5.für _____ Kalendar (masc.)
6.für ____ Geschäft (the business; neuter)
7.fur _____ Studentin

The Dative

Here are the dative endings:

	masculine	feminine	neuter	plural
Nominative	der	die	das	die
Accusative	den	die	das	die
Dative	dem	der	dem	den

The prepositions mit and seit take the dative case.

Provide the correct for of the definite article (der/die/das/den/dem etc.):

1. mit _____ Mann
2. mit _____ Projekt (neut.)
3. seit _____ Jahr 2012 (neut.)
4. mit _____ Frau (this may look odd but check the chart above for dative feminine)
5. mit _____ Computer

Months of the year

Der Endtermin ist im Januar. — the final deadline is in January.

Notice that Termin can mean appointment or deadline.

Also note that you say <u>am</u> Montag, but <u>im</u> Januar.

Der Endtermin ist im Januar
im Februar
im März
im April
im Mai
im Juni
im Juli
im August
im September
im Oktober
im November
im Dezember

When? / Wann ist ... ? Answer with a full sentence, but just give the month, not the date: ...im März, etc.

1. Wann ist Weihnachten?
2. Wann ist Halloween?
3. Wann ist Ihr Geburtstag? (your birthday)
4. Wann ist Fasching? (Mardi gras)
5. Wann ist Sommer? (summer)
6. Wann ist Oktoberfest?
7. Wann ist Advent?

Dialog

Ich kenne Sie nicht. Seit wann arbeiten Sie hier?
Seit einer Woche. Ich heiße Kevin.
Seit einer Woche? Willkommen. Werden Sie gut angeleitet?
Ja, sehr gut, danke.

kennen – to know a person or a city; wissen – to know a fact
seit wann – since when
seit + Dativ – since
Werden Sie gut angeleitet? - Are you being well integrated into the company? (This is a German cultural concept)

Dialog

(walking in late to a meeting:)
Ich komme spät, es tut mir leid.
Das ist gar kein Problem. Ich kenne Sie nicht. Sind Sie neu bei uns?
Ja, seit einer Woche. Ich heiße Kevin Bachmann.
Willkommen und setzten Sie sich bitte.

spät – late
gar kein – not at all
bei uns – at our company (can also mean at our house or home)
setzten Sie sich bitte – please take a seat

Dialog

Komme ich zu spät?
Gar nicht. Sie kommen pünktlich. Es ist erst 11 Uhr.
Was werden wir heute diskutieren?
Wir diskutieren gerade neue Projekte.

pünktlich – on time, punctual
erst – only (in time expressions)
(nur="only" in all other situations)
Was werden wir diskutieren? – What are we going to discuss?
Projekte – projects, the plural of Projekt

Plurals

feminine plurals are usually —en but there are MANY exceptions, masculine plurals are usually —e but there are even more exceptions, and neuter plurals can be —e, -er, Umlaut plus —er, Umlaut plus —e, just an Umlaut, the same as the singular form, or a range of other possibilities. For beginning students, it's best to learn the plurals of common words, especially nouns that often come in the plural such as "die Schuhe," "shoes."

Kultur

For many German, the intimate "du" form is reserved for family and close friends who are accepted as though they were family. Other Germans say "du" at the drop of a hat. This can be confusing to foreigners. Please note that online usage, especially if anonymous, is sometimes du (for example, in a forum about technical matters), even with strangers, but if the conversations goes offline, you may switch to Sie. Some very close friends call each other Sie for their entire lives, and some people use du upon first meeting. As one German puts it, "It has to feel right. You can't establish rules for this."

Germans have an equally confusing array of words for friendship. A Kumpel is a pal or buddy, but may or may not be close. Some pals are kept at arm's length, others are close friends. A German may have Kumpels that he sees every day at a Kneipe (a pub) but would never call friends. Freund is a meaningful word, intimating closeness, so that phrases such as "treuer Freund" and "enger Freund" are almost tautological. Facebook has re-positioned the word "Freund" but many Germans see Facebook as an exception: an English or American use of the word friend. Bekannte is the term for an aquaintance and simply means "one who is known to me," and is a stronger bond than the English equivalent.

Kapitel 5
Das sind online-meetings

- English expressions
- Gender of English words
- Basic computer and IT vocabulaty
- The genitive case
- How Germans view non-Germans

Business-Englisch (note the spelling of Englisch) is a predominant form of how Germans have reached out to the world community, but when Germans are speaking German, the English lexicon is very teutonically nuanced.

For example, computer is der Computer, the plural is die Computer, the genitive (not the plural) is Computers, and the dative plural is Computern.

Zeitmanagement is a common words, and all Germans strive for Business-Kenntnis. (Kenntnis=know-how). The truth is, German business is largely conducted in German, with a sprinkling of English words that can baffle native speakers on both sides of the German-English divide. Let's get started.

die Seite — the page
die Webseite — the webpage
die Hauptseite — the main page/index page
auf der Webseite — on the webpage (der is a feminine dative)

Dialog

Diese Firma (company) "Neusoft" hat keine Webseite.

Doch, doch. Ich habe ihre Webseite besucht (I have visited their webpage).

Stimmt schon. Ich bin jetzt auf der Hauptseite. Ich brauche Kontaktinformation und eine Faxnummer.

Ist die Faxnummer auf der Hauptseite?

Ja, ja. Das Pulldown-Menü hat die Faxnummer.

doch, doch – on the contrary
ich brauche – I need
auf - on

das Menü is a computer menu, not a menu in a restaurant.

Matching Column

1. auf der Webseite	a) scroll down
2. brauchen	b) good skills, know-how
3. die Datenbank	
4. das Management	c) in the pulldown menu
5. die Nummer	
6. gute Kenntnisse	d) to need
7. runterscrollen	e) with computers
8. in dem Computer	f) on the website
9. in dem Pulldown-Menü	g) in the computer
	h) the database
10. mit Computern	i) number
	j) management

Dative

Remember that some prepositions take the dative?

in dem Computer (in + dative)
in dem Pulldown-Menü
in der Webseite

Dative: dem for masc. and neut.; der for feminine

Fill in dem or der:

1. auf ____Webseite
2. in ___ Computer
3. auf _____Festplatte (fem.)
4. in _____ Pulldown-Menü (neut.)
5. in ___ Code (masc.)

Contractions

in dem Computer = im Computer (both phrases are correct, im Computer is more usual)

Matching column

1. der Code, die Maus, das Menü	a. data
2. vor	b. two meanings: in front of OR before
3. die Festplatte	
4. was denn?	c. upload, dowload
5. laden	d. load
6. hochladen, herunterladen	e. what then?
7. Daten	f. hard drive
	g. code, mouse, menu

ihr = their:
ihre Festplatte – their hard drive
Ihr (capitalized) = Your;
Was ist Ihr Name? Ich heiße Rudolf.

Dialog

Wo ist meine Maus?
Da, vor dem Computer.
Gut, gut. Ich möchte vor der Besprechung etwas
(something) machen.
Was denn?
Ich möchte Daten herunterladen.
Sind die Daten nicht auf Ihrer Hard-Drive?
Hard-Drive? Was ist das?
Entschuldigung (pardon). Ihre Festplatte.
Auf der Festplatte? Nein, leider nicht. Die daten
sind im „Cloud."

Leider nicht – unfortunately not
herunterladen – download
herunterscrollen – scroll down
hochladen – upload
aufscrollen – scroll up
vor der Besprechung – before the meeting
vor dem Computer – in front of the computer
(vor has two meanings)

Dialog

Wo ist mein Bunutzerhandbuch?
Da, auf dem Computer.
Gut, gut. Ich werde es heute brauchen.
Warum denn?
Ich muss neuen Code schreiben.

Benutzer – user
auf dem Computer – on top of the computer
Ich werde es brauchen – I will need it
ich muss – I have to

Verb infinitives reminder

Ich kann + Verb Infinitive
Ich werde + Verb Infinitive
Ich muss + Verb Infinitive

Dialog

Wo ist Ihre Maus?
Da, vor meinem Computer. Warum fragen Sie?
Ich brauche sie. Darf ich sie nehmen (take)?
Wieso? Haben Sie keine Maus?
Nein ich habe keine. Ich schreibe meistens Code.
Ich benutze (use) meistens keine Maus.
Was schreiben Sie im Moment?
Das Benutzerinterface.

Verb list:
nehmen – to take
brauchen – to need
benutzen - to use

Guess the meanings:

der Endbenutzer
das Benutzerinterface
das Benutzerhandbuch

Translate:

1. I have to take your Laptop. (der Laptop, ich muss..)

2. I will need a new hard drive. (eine neue Festplatte)

Hint: use Ich werde....

Festplatte is an exampe of a word that most people understand in German, but few Germans would recognize the word „hard drive." Thus, hard drive really has not become a German word. Festplatte is strongly preferred in German. It is short for Festplattenlaufwerk, which is also something that non-technical Germans may not know!

Let's re-visit and re-tool our earlier **Dialog**ue: Please note: „noch" means „still, yet, it's still the case that...."

Dialog

Wo ist meine Maus? Ich habe so viel Zeug auf meinem Schreibtisch.
Da, vor dem Computer. Unter dem Benutzerhandbuch.
Gut, gut. Ich möchte vor der Besprechung etwas noch tun. (tun=machen)
Was denn? Die Besprechung fängt gleich an.
Ich möchte einige Daten herunterladen und ausdrucken.
Sind die Daten nicht auf Ihrer Festplatte?
Nein, leider nicht. Die daten sind noch im Cloud.

so viel Zeug – so much stuff
Ich muss etwas noch tun – I still have to do something
fängt gleich an – is about to begin
Daten – data
ausdrucken – to print out

Dialog

Guten Tag, ich möchte einen Laptop kaufen.
Gut. Was für eine Speicherkapazität brauchen
Sie?
Ich weiß es nicht.

Speicherkapazität – storage capacity
speichern – to store
was für ein – what kind of a
„of the computer," „of the hard drive," „of the
website"

The possessive case is called the genitive.

des Computers – of the computer
des Büros – of the office
des Unternehmens – of the company

Was ist der Name des Unternehmens?
Was ist die Speicherkapazität des Computers?

**Change the following phrases from „the handbook" to „of the handbook" etc.
(use des....-s)**

1. das Handbuch
2. der Benutzer
3. der Code
4. das Management

Translate:

What is the language (die Sprache) of the code?

„Der Benutzer" in the genitive case is....des Benutzers

Using des ....-s works for masculine and neuter nouns. Feminine nouns are different.

Let's fill in the chart of German cases so far.

	masculine	feminine	neuter	plural
Nominative	der	die	das	die
Accusative	den	die	das	die
Dative	dem	der	dem	den
Genitive	des		des	

Or perhaps it would be more accurate to say:

	masculine	feminine	neuter	plural
Nominative	der	die	das	die
Accusative	den	die	das	die
Dative	dem	der	dem	den
Genitive	des....-s		des...-s	

Take the phrase „der Computer" and write it in the four cases:

Nominative	
Accusative	
Dative	
Genitive	

Translate:

What is the storage capacity of the computer?

Can you fill in the empty column below?

	What is it used for?	masc	fem	neut	plur
Nominative		der	die	das	die
Accusative		den	die	das	die
Dative		dem	der	dem	den
Genitive		des		des	

Your answers should look like this:

	What is it used for?	
Nominative	the subject of a verb	
Accusative	the direct object of a verb OR after some prepositions	
Dative	after some prepositions	
Genitive	It means „of the" (in other words, it shows possession)	

„of the" (Genitive case)

the condition of the desk is chaos:
Der Zustand <u>des Schreibtisches</u> ist ein Chaos.

So...how do you say „of the" for feminine nouns? Notice that the feminine box is empty above.

„of the website"
Die Beta-Version <u>der Webseite</u> ist sehr interessant.

„of the boss (feminine)"
Die Meinung (opinion) <u>der Chefin</u> ist sehr positiv.

der Webseite – of the website
der Besprechung – of the meeting
des Planes – of the plan (masc.)
der Chefin – of the boss (fem.)

Here is the complete chart for German case:

	masculine	feminine	neuter	plural
Nominative	der	die	das	die
Accusative	den	die	das	die
Dative	dem	der	dem	den
Genitive	des	der	des	der

Here are the uses for the cases:

Nominative	the subject of a verb
Accusative	the direct object of a verb OR after some prepositions
Dative	the indirect object OR after some prepositions
Genitive	It means „of the" (in other words, it shows possession) OR after some prepositions

Kultur

How do Germans view non-Germans? For one thing, Austrians and the Swiss people have very similar culture and language and except for a sense of regionalism (that also exists within Germany), all three nations in many ways view each other as sharing a single culture.

Like many proud nations, Germans see their own culture as advantageous and may have trouble understanding the reasoning behind other ways of doing things. There is a sense that the German way is "natural."

Germany is also a nation that lacks clear natural boundaries, and itself borders on nine other nations. Except for language and culture, it's hard to say what defines Germans. Germans travel extensively, speak foreign languages, and are aware of world events. Expect a cosmopolitain world view, but with a quiet assumption that it would have made more sense for the peoples around the world to be more similar to Germans.

Beware of injudiciously phrased comments, which can seem like cultural insensitivity. There is an anthropological naivete to the Germans' view of others, but Germans also have an openness and often a disarming kindness when encountering non-Germans.

Kapitel 6
Wie war Ihre Reise?

- Business travel and conferences
- The past tense
- sein versus haben in the perfect tense
- Alles in Ordnung?
- German cleanliness, categories and cubicles

Wohin sind Sie gereist?

Ich bin letztes Jahr nach Deutschland geflogen.

Where did you travel to?

I flew to Germany last year.

Dialog

Guten Morgen, Jürgen.
Servus.
Also, Sie fliegen nach Hannover?
Ja, heute Nachmittag.
Haben wir Kunden in Hannover?
Nein, es gibt eine Konferenz.
Gute Reise also.
Ja, danke sehr.

also – so...
fliegen – to fly
Nachmittag – afternoon
Kunden – customers
Es gibt – there is or there are
Gute Reise – have a good trip

der Kunde – customer (male)
die Kund_in_ – customer (female)

Kunden- customers

Kundenservice – customer service

Dialog

Haben wir Kunden in München?
Ja, mehrere Kunden sogar.
Kann ich unsere Software präsentieren?
Ja, warum denn nicht.
Gut. Ich muss nächsten Donnerstag nach München
fahren.
Warum? Gibt es eine Konferenz?
Nein. Meine Lieblingsband spielt in der
Konzerthalle in München.

spielt- is playing
mehrere – several
sogar – even, in fact, as it happens
Lieblings-Band – favorite band

Dialog

Ich muss nächsten Donnerstag nach Berlin fahren.
Warum? Gibt es eine Konferenz?
Nein. Meine Tochter (daughter) spielt in der
Konzerthalle.

Matching column
use leo.org as needed

1. reisen	a. identification
2. Reisebüro	b. everything is ready
3. der Flughafen	c. check in
4. fliegen	d. airline tickets
5. Koffer packen	e. to travel
6. alles ist bereit	f. fly
7. Flugtickets	g. visa
8. einchecken	h. travel agency
9. der Pass	i. passport
10. der Ausweis	j. airport (flight-haven)
11. das Visum	k. packen suitcases

Dialog

Gehen Sie zur Besprechung?
Ja und dann fliege ich nach Berlin.
Sie fliegen nach Berlin?
Ja, Sie haben meine Reise gebucht, oder?
Nein, ich habe vergessen.

zur= zu der (to the)
Ich habe die Reise gebucht – I booked the travel
ich habe vergessen – I forgot

Dialog

Ist das Ihr Gepäck, Herr Reinke?
Ja, das ist Handgepäck.
Haben Sie nichts mehr?
Nein, der Rücksack ist alles.
Aber Sie bleiben sieben Tage in Russland.
Ja, ich gehe wandern.
Okay, jetzt verstehe ich.

Hand-Gepäck — carry-on-luggage
Rücksack — backpack
alles — everything
nichts — nothing
bleiben — stay, remain
wandern - hiking
ich verstehe — I understand

„I understand now."
You can say:

Ich verstehe jetzt.
or
Jetzt verstehe ich.

Just make sure the verb is in the second position.

Dialog

Ich fahre nach Irland. Kennen Sie Irland?
Ja so ein bisschen. Ich habe Dublin und Galway
besucht.
Können Sie mir ein paar Tipps geben?
Ja, wollen wir ein Bier trinken?
Gut. Ich lade Sie auf ein Bier ein.

ein bisschen – a little bit
ich habe Dublin besucht – I visited Dublin
mir-to me
wollen wir- do we want to?
Ich lade Sie auf ein Bier ein – I'll buy you a
beer.

Dialog

Fliegen Sie diese Woche nach Japan?
Ja, morgen schon. Ich besuche Kunden in Tokio.
Waren Sie schon mal in Japan?
Nein. Noch nie.
Und die Kunden sprechen Deutsch?
Ein bisschen Deutsch und ein bisschen Englisch.
Und ich spreche kein Japanisch.
Ich habe viele Bilder von der Marketing-
Abteilung. Bilder sind immer gut.

schon – already
nie=niemals (never)
immer- always
Waren Sie schon mal? – Were you already?
Bilder – pictures
die Abteilung – the department

Ich habe gesehen – I saw
Ich habe besucht – I visited
Ich habe Deutsch gesprochen – I spoke German
Sie haben einen Termin gemacht.
Florian hat ein Auto gekauft. (purchased)

To make the past tense, use:

a helping verb (haben) plus a Past participle

Do the past participles on the previous page look similar to each other? Is there any kind of pattern?

Matching column

1. Ich habe einen Termin ....   a. gewohnt
2. Ich habe ein bisschen   b. gesehen
   Deutsch....   c. gelernt
3. Ich habe das Kathedral in Ulm d. gemacht
   ...
4. Ich habe in Stuttgart .....

The past tense is made by using the stem of the verb

(wohn- from wohnen):

| Ich | a conjugated helping verb (usually haben) | + | ge (verb)+ -t or -en |

The last part (the past participle that begins with ge-) goes at the end of the sentence.

Translate

1. I lived in München.
2. I learned German.
3. I saw Oktoberfest.

Dialog

Haben Sie die neue Software gesehen?
Die Beta-Version von Januar, ja.
Nein, es gibt heute eine neue Version.
Gut! Nein, ich habe sie nicht gesehen.
Haben Sie Ihre Email gelesen?
Nein, ich war in einer Besprechung.

von –from
ich war – I was
gesehen – (have) seen
gelesen – (have) read

Alles in Ordnung?

Is everything in good order?

Dialog

Wann kommen die Kunden aus Norwegen?
Um 14 Uhr.
Ist alles bereit?
Ja, die Marketing-Abteilung hat die
Präsentation bereit.
Gut. Dieser Besuch ist sehr wichtig für uns.

bereit – ready
sehr wichtig – very important

In the past tense the helping verb can sometimes
be sein

sein-to be (I am, you are, he is, etc.)

ich bin	wir sind
du bist	ihr seid
er/sie/es ist	sie sind, Sie sind

The past tense:

| Ich (or du, er, Hans, Stephanie, any subject of the verb) | haben OR sein

This is the helping verb, and it gets conjugated | + | ge (verb)+ -t or —en

(Sometimes there's no ge-) |

Ich habe einen Film gesehen.
Ich habe einen Computer gekauft.

but:

Ich <u>bin</u> nach Hannover gefahren.

This verb (fahren) takes sein instead of haben as its helping verb in the past tense.

Translate:

1. I drove to München.
2. I saw Oktoberfest.
3. I sang „Ein Prosit" in German. (auf Deutsch; habe...gesungen)
4. I drove back to Regensburg. (zurück=back)

When you write in the past tense, begin each sentence with Ich habe... (or Ich bin....)

_____

_____

_____

_____

_____

_____

_____

_____

_____

_____

_____

_____

verb	past tense
sehen	habe gesehen
wohnen	habe gewohnt
fahren	*bin gefahren
fliegen	*bin geflogen
landen (to land a plane)	habe gelandet
relaxen	habe relaxt
chillen	habe gechillt

Write a paragraph using at least three past tenses from the chart above.

_____

_____

_____

_____

Dialog

(am Telephon)
Sind Sie im Hotel?
Ja, ich bin nach Frankfurt geflogen und dann nach Wiesbaden.
Alles in Ordnung?
Ja, das Hotel ist schön. Ich habe gegessen. (I have eaten)
Arbeiten Sie jetzt am Laptop?
Nein, nein, ich habe ein bisschen relaxt, das ist alles.
Gut. Ihre Präsentation morgen ist sehr wichtig. Haben Sie die PowerPoints?
Ja, auf der Festplatte und ich habe zwei Siicherheitskopien (back-up copies) gemacht.
Gut! Ja, alles in Ordnung. Okay, viel Glück morgen.
Danke sehr. Bis Freitag also.
Ja. Auf wiederhören.

Past Tense of WEAK VERBS

„Weak" verbs are essentially those verbs that have past participles that end in –t (rather than –en)

The past tense:

Subject of the verb	haben	+	ge (verb stem)+ -t
	(or sein for a verb of motion or a change in condition)		(There's no ge- if the verb stem contains an inseparable prefix)

lernen – ich habe ein bisschen Deutsch gelernt

wohnen – ich habe in Paderborn gewohnt

sagen – ich habe "ja" gesagt

hoffen – ich habe gehofft, dass..

rechnen – ich habe die Nummer gerechnet

Which phrase on the previous page means what?
said-learned-calculated-hoped-lived

Some verbs that shows motion or a change in condition take "sein" as their helping verb in the past tense:

reisen – ich <u>bin</u> gereist (because it's a verb of motion)

Some verbs in German have a prefix that is inseparably part of the verb stem. be- / ver- / ent- / er- are examples.

Ich habe den Kunden begrüßt – I greeted the customer

Notice that there is no ge- in the past participle "begrüßt." Another example is erledigen – to do a task:

Ich habe die Arbeit erledigt – I completed the work

Any verb that ends in –ieren will also not have a ge- in the past tense:

Ich habe Marketing an der Uni studiert – I studied marketing at university

Frau Klempner hat das Projekt finanziert.

Past Tense of STRONG VERBS

„Strong" verbs are essentially those verbs that have past participles that end in –en (rather than –t)
Strong verbs also show a lot of other irregularities in their verb stems when it comes to the past tense.

Strong verbs are a more ancient kind of German verb, and the irregular changes are remnants from a time when the past tense was made in different ways. Please see my other writings to learn more about this if you are interested.

The past tense of strong verbs:

Subject of the verb	haben (or **sein** for a verb of motion or a change in condition)	+	ge (verb stem) + -en
			The verb stem often has changes and irregularities
			There's no ge- if the verb stem contains an inseparable prefix

sprechen – Ich habe mit einem Kollegen **gesprochen**

helfen – ich habe dem Kunden **geholfen**

finden – ich habe den Jahresbericht (annual report) **gefunden**

essen – ich habe in der Kantine (cafeteria at work) **gegessen**

geben -ich habe dem Kunden einen Prospekt (advertising flyer) **gegeben**

Some verbs that shows motion or a change in condition take "sein" as their helping verb in the past tense:

gehen – **ich <u>bin</u> gegangen** (because it's a verb of motion)

fahren – **ich <u>bin</u> gefahren**
fliegen – **ich <u>bin</u> geflogen**

Some strong verbs in German have a prefix that is inseparably part of the verb stem and takes the place of ge-:

Ich habe etwas vergessen – I forgot something

Wir haben die Daten verloren – We lost the data

Ich habe eine Email bekommen – I received an email

Choose 15 useful verbs for Business German. Go to leo.org to find the German translation. Then go to de.wictionary.org to find the past tense (look in the chart under: Perfekt tense).

	dict.leo.org	de.wictionary.org
to purchase	kaufen	habe gekauft

kreatives Schreiben
Using leo and de.wictionary, write an imaginary story in the past tense with a business backdrop. Use extra paper as needed.

_____

_____

_____

_____

_____

_____

_____

_____

_____

_____

_____

_____

_____

_____

_____

Kultur

It is a stereotype, but it also happens to be true: Germans have a preference for orderliness, well-organized spaces, and efficient and logical organization systems.

When interacting with Germans in a business setting, avoid any presentations or materials to distribute that could be interpreted as sloppy or disorderly. What might seem spontaneous and fun in one culture could possibly be seen as disorderly -- unordentlich -- to Germans.

Germans believe in the motto of following an orderly procedure. In other cultures, we might take shortcuts in order to meet an important deadline, but Germans are hesitant to sacrifice procedure for product. This is both extremely advantageous and occasionally disadvantageous. Try to work harmoniously with the German mindset, and understand the importance of order as a cultural value.

116

Only two basic grammatical concepts remain and both will be covered in Chapter 7: reflexive verbs and separable-prefix verbs.

Of the English examples below, which do you think are reflexive verbs and which are separable-prefix verbs?

Herr Becker, what time are you planning to wake up?

Herr Jung, please come in and seat yourself. Help yourself to coffee and cake.

Answer: reflexive verbs include to seat oneself and to help oneself; separable-prefix verbs include to wake up and to come in

Kapitel 7
Der Arbeitstag

- The workday from dawn to Feierabend
- Separable prefix verbs
- Reflexive verbs
- Inviting a colleague for coffee
- Family vocabulary
- Statistics about the average German

Dialog

Es ist Feierabend.
Ich habe heute sehr wenig gemacht.
Lassen Sie die Arbeit. Sie haben genug getan.
Ja, aber die Kunden kommen schon am Mittwoch an.
Das hat noch Zeit. Kommen Sie.
Aber meine Präsentation ist nicht fertig.
Lassen Sie das. Der Arbeitstag ist fertig.

Feierabend — the end of the workday
sehr wenig — very little
Lassen Sie es — leave it
fertig — done with, over with

Dialog

Feierabend, Gerhard.
Ich arbeite an einem wichtigen Projekt.
Si können bleiben, ich gehe jezt nach Hause.

wichtig — important
bleiben — to stay, remain

Dialog

Ich arbeite an einem Projekt und ich möchte früh
am Morgen wieder anfangen.
Um wie viel Uhr wollen Sie ankommen?
Um 5 oder halb 6.
Gut, ich sage Frank Bescheid. Er wird hier sein.
Danke.
An welchem Projekt arbeiten Sie?
Software für die Kunden aus Canada.

anfangen – begin
ankommen – arrive
Er wird hier sein – He will be here
ich werde, er wird – (an irregular verb); the
future tense

Dialog

Feierabend, Markus.
Endlich. Das war ein langer Tag.
Das Wetter ist schön. Ich werde hier einen
Spaziergang machen bevor ich nach Hause
fahre.
Ich komme mit. Ich brauche ein bisschen Luft.
Sie werden mitkommen? Gut, wir können das
Canada-Projekt diskutieren.
Nein. Es ist Feierabend. Lassen Sie die Arbeit.

einen Spaziergang machen – go for a walk
mitkommen – to come along

Matching column

1. ankommen	a. prepare
2. mitmachen	b. call, telephone
3. anfangen	c. arrive
4. anrufen	d. take along
5. einladen	e. participate
6. vorbereiten	f. begin
7. mitnehmen	g. invite

We have already seen inseparable prefix verbs, in which the verb prefix is an integral part of the verb.

For the verbs above, the prefixes (an- / mit- /vor- / ein-) are <u>separable</u>. They can be separated from the rest of the verb.

Ich <u>lade</u> Sie auf einen Kaffee <u>ein</u>. – I'm inviting you for a coffee.

Ich <u>lade</u> die Daten <u>hoch</u>. – I'm uploading the data.

ein-laden and hoch-laden mean completely different things because of the different prefixes.

Ich <u>rufe</u> den Kunden sofort <u>an</u> – I'll telephone the customer right away.

The prefix in these examples goes to the end of the sentence, but it is still part of the verb.

After Ich kann...,

ich muss..., and ich werde...:

Ich werde Sie auf ein Bier <u>einladen</u>, wenn die Arbeit fertig ist.

I will invite you for a beer when the work is done

In the past tense (Perfekt), these verbs have a – ge- infix between the prefix and the past participle of the verb stem:

Ich habe mein Handgepäck <u>mit**ge**nommen</u>.

Ich habe Karl auf ein Bier <u>ein**ge**laden</u>.

Haben Sie den Kunden <u>an**ge**rufen</u>?

Dialog

Sie haben eine Familie?
Ja, ich bin verheiratet und ich habe zwei Kinder.
Wie alt sind Ihre Kinder?
Mein Sohn Sebastian ist vierzehn und meine
Tochter Amilia ist erst zwölf.
Ich habe auch einen Sohn. Er ist fünfzehn Jahre
alt.
Sind Sie verheiratet?
Ja, meine Frau ist auch Ingenieurin wie ich.
Und Sie haben nur das eine Kind?
Ja. Er heißt Nathan.

verheiratet – married
Sohn, Tochter, Ehemann, Ehefrau – son,
daughter, husband, wife
Ingenieur – engineer
nur das eine Kind – only the one child
Haben Sie eine Familie?
When asking about family, be friendly but not intrusive. A casual emark such as "Tell me about your family" is acceptable in English-speaking cultures but seems prying to a German. Talking about family is an invitation to friendly conversation, but it is a not a superficial topic or small talk – not for Germans

Dialog

Was haben Sie bisher gesehen?
Nichts. Die Software sieht gut aus.
Keine Probleme?
Bisher nicht.

bisher – up until now, so far
sieht gut aus – looks good

Dialog

Was haben Sie bisher gemacht?
Ich bin um 8 Uhr angekommen und ich habe den
ganzen Morgen Code geschrieben.
Ist das nicht langweilig?
Ich arbeit gern fokussiert an einem Projekt.
Ich arbeite lieber an mehreren Projekten.

langweilig – dull
lieber – I prefer
mehrere – several

Dialog

Endlich mal. Mich hinsetzen und einen Kaffee trinken.

Was haben Sie bisher gemacht?

Ich bin um 7 Uhr angekommen und ich habe mit dem Jahresbericht (annual report) angefangen. Herr Lehmann hat angerufen und ich habe ihm eine Email mit Marketing-Daten geschickt. Herr Frank hat mich gesehen und wollte eine Besprechung vereinbaren.

Alles in Ordnung?

Ja, alles geht gut aber mir ist es lieber wenn ich fokussiert an einem Projekt arbeite, nicht alles auf einmal.

wollte — wanted to

alles auf einmal — everything at once

The two past tenses. The **Perfekt** is the two-part past tense that we have been learning and it the more common past tense in speaking. The **Präteritum** is a one-word past tense that often has similarities to the past participles.

"ich war" and "ich wollte" are examples of the Präteritum.

Dialog

Sind die PowerPoints fertig?
Noch nicht. Ich habe die Bilder nicht eingefügt.
Aber der Text ist fertig?
Der Text ist fertig.
Schon gut. Die Kunden sind hier. Sie sind früher
als erwartet angekommen.

fertig – finished, done
Bilder-pictures
einfügen – to add
schon gut – that's good already, good enough
früh – early
früher als erwartet – earlier than expected
ankommen – to arrive (takes sein in the past
tense)

Matching Column

1. angekommen	a. telephoned
2. eingefügt	b. participated
3. mitgemacht	c. invited
4. eingeladen	d. began
5. mitgenommen	e. assumed
6. angesprochen	f. arrived
7. angefangen	g. approached and
8. angerufen	spoke to
9. angenommen	h. added
	i. took along, carried

Dialog

Alles in Ordnung?
Nicht genau. Der Computer ist abgestürzt.
Schon wieder?
Ja, ich weiß nicht warum.
Rufen Sie Herrn Becker an.

genau — exactly
abstürzen — to crash
schon — already
wieder — again
anrufen — to call
ich weiß nicht — I don't know

Dialog

Der Computer ist abgestürzt.
Haben Sie Herrn Becker angerufen?
Nein, noch nicht. (not yet)

Dialog

Alles in Ordnung?
Meine Frau hat angerufen. Mein Sohn ist krank.
Müssen Sie nach Hause fahren?
Nein, meine Frau macht das heute.
Wie alt ist Ihr Sohn?
Vierzehn aber er spielt Fußball wie ein Profi.

Dialog

Können wir das neue Projekt diskutieren?
Ich habe keine Zeit. Können Sie mit David
sprechen?
David ist nach Hause gegangen.
Sprechen Sie mit Silvia. Sie wird eine
Besprechung vereinbaren.

ich werde, du wirst, er/sie wird

(irregular verb that creates the future tense)

Giving orders.

Sprechen Sie mit Silvia – speak with Silvia.
Geben Sie mir den Bericht – Give me the report.

To create an imperative verb form (a command), use the infinitive plus the word Sie.

<u>**Kommen Sie**</u> **bitte zur** (=zu der/to the) **Besprechung.**
<u>**Rufen Sie**</u> **Herrn Becker an.**

Dialog

Wann kommt der Lieferer an (supplier)?
Um 14 Uhr.
Und wann kommt der Kunde an?
Um 11 Uhr.
Das ist ein Problem.

Dialog

Sind Sie verheiratet?
Ja, und ich habe drei Kinder.
Ich bin verheiratet aber ich habe keine Kinder.
Sowohl meine Mutter als auch die Mutter meiner
Frau wohnen bei uns.
Zwei Omas. Die Kinder haben es gut.
Ja, und die Cousins wohnen im Nebenhous.
Meine Schwester ist auch verheiratet.
Mein Bruder ist verheiratet. Ich habe eine Nichte.

die Nichte-niece
die Mutter meiner Frau — the mother of my wife
Bruder,Schwester,Oma — brother, sister,
grandmother
das Nebenhaus — the house next door

Reflexive verbs

Ich arbeite is a simple, non-reflexive verb: "I work."

Ich **entspanne mich** is a reflexive verb: "I relax" or more literally: I'm relaxing <u>myself</u>

Ich **setze mich** – I'm seating myself, I'm sitting down

sich setzen – to seat oneself	
ich setze mich	wir setzen uns
du setzt dich	ihr setzt euch
er/sie/es setzt sich	sie setzen sich, Sie setzen sich

sich beeilen – to hurry oneself

Ich muss mich beeilen – I have to hurry.
Warum beeilen Sie sich? – Why are you hurrying yourself?

Visit Leo.org to check the pronunciation of beeilen. It's tricky. Be- is a prefix and –eilen sounds like "island"

German has many reflexive verbs. Many verbs are reflexive in German but not in English.

sich entscheiden – to decide, literally: "to decide ~~oneself~~"

Entscheiden Sie sich bitte! – Please decide!

Beeilen Sie sich bitte! – Please hurry up!

Dialog

Ist die Auto-CAD-Graphik fertig?
Fertig? Ich habe das noch nicht angefangen.
Beeilen Sie sich bitte!

die Graphik – diagram
noch nicht – not yet
anfangen - begin
sich beeilen – to hurry up

Dialog

Ist die PowerPoint-Präsentation fertig?
Der Text ist fertig aber ich habe noch keine
Bilder eingefügt.
Beeilen Sie sich bitte!

Bilder einfügen — to add (insert) pictures

Dialog

Was machen Sie da? Die PowerPoints?
Nein, ich konzentriere mich auf die AutoCAD-
Graphik.

da-there
sich konzentrieren + auf — to focus on

Advanced German:

Some verbs are reflexive AND separable prefix. These can be challenging.

sich vor-stellen — to introduce - oneself
sich vor-bereiten — to get prepared

Stellen Sie sich vor — Please introduce yourself

Bereiten Sie sich vor — Be prepared, Get ready

Dialog

Harald, stellen Sie sich bitte vor. (introduce yourself)
Mein Name ist Harald Reinke. Ich komme aus Wiesbaden. Ich arbeite in der Marketing-Abteilung. Ich arbeite schon sieben Jahre hier bei der Firma.

in der Abteilung (fem.) — in the department
schon — already
hier bei der Firma — here at this company

Dialog

Wann kommen die Kunden?
Um 15 Uhr.
Bereiten Sie sich gut vor. Ihre Präsentation ist wichtig.
Sie ist fertig und ich habe auch eine AutoCAD-Graphik gemacht.
Schöne Arbeite. Ich sehe, Sie haben sich schon gut vorbereitet.

Kultur

According to the work of Jean-Remy von Matt, who co-founded the "Jung von Matt" advertising agency in Hamburg, the average German couple has 1.4 children. The average German wakes up at 6.23 am. and begins work at 7.49 am. The most common last name is Müller and among first names, the most common are Thomas and Sabine.

100 million Europeans speak German, making it the most commonly spoken language in the European Union. With a population of 82.3 million, Germany is the most populous nation in the European Union.

The telephone prefix is +49. and the Day of National Unity, October 3, celebrates the Reunification of West and East Germany. The tallest mountain is the Zugspitze, at 2,963 meters. With 357,021 square km. of land, Germany has only 2,389 km of coastline.

53 million people claim religious affiliation and pay religion tax. Of these, it is striking that 26 million are Catholic and 26 million are Protestant: a legacy of the winner-less 30 Years' War of the 17th Century between Protestants and Catholics. There is no state religion but also no separation of church and state. Religion classes are common in schools.

The largest cities are Berlin, Hamburg, München, Köln and Frankfurt, in that order.

Germany is the world's leading exporter and its largest trading partner is France, which purchases 9.5% of Germany's exports by volume.

70% of Germans work for a mid-sized company, giving the German workforce a unique profile. Germans own more patents than any other Europeans, and after the USA and Japan, rank third in terms of total number of patents.

160 major world fairs take place in Germany. More text is translated both into and out of German than any other nation on the planet.

Are you ready for the next challenge? Business German textbooks from Kuhn and Neuss Publishers come in a variety of levels: beginner, advanced beginner, intermediate, high intermediate, and intermediate/advanced. In the pages ahead you will find a sample of the intermediate/advanced level textbook.

1 der Profi

Chapter 1 explores communicating and thinking like a German professional. New expressions include *taking the initiative, showing someone the ropes, thinking in a professional way, enjoying your work,* and *getting promoted.* Topics include job fulfillment, the first day at work, and how old and new come together in German business.

2 Teamarbeit

This chapter explores teamwork and team building—what does a team look like when it is working smoothly? Why do Germans place so much value on effective and efficient teamwork, and how do they achieve it?

3 Pack's an

An important aspect of managing a successful professional career in any field is how to map out the steps involved in completing a project. This chapter asks the question: "How will you proceed?" New expressions include tackling a project, taking the first steps, managing ongoing projects, developing a road map, etc.

4 ungezwungen

Being too casual with German colleagues is still a common mistake; nonetheless, a new style has set in, and many German workplaces embrace a far more casual approach to communications than in recent years. This chapter explores a changing work environment and the new "business casual."

5 zocken texten surfen

This chapter is about workplace technologies, communication, and technology use in free time. Students can discuss how they use technology, and talk about what is appropriate in the workplace, particularly the German workplace, as well as how technologies support work processes and day-to-day life.

6 das Bewerbungsgespräch

Almost every university student is preparing for his/her first job interview. This chapter discusses strategies, common mistakes, German expectations, and how to stand out from the crowd. A sample job interview walks students through what it means to answer questions effectively and to go through an interview with an understanding for what employers are looking for.

7 Zeit ist Geld

"Pfeilschnell ist das Jetzt entflogen" (" 'Now' is gone, quick as an arrow"/Friedrich Schiller) and nowhere does this maxim hold truer than in a busy workplace. This chapter is about managing a challenging workload. The language of chapter 7 is more complex than in the pre-vious chapters. Expressions include putting a project aside, being under constant time pressure, work-flow management, time blocking, and getting a handle on the workload.

Nur im Deutschen sagt man:

„Arbeit macht das Leben süß"

Rollenspiel: Schreiben Sie mit Ihrem/mit Ihrer Partner(in) einen Dialog, der mit der Phrase „Arbeit mach das Leben süß!" endet.

Gedankenanstöße:
Pessimist und Optimist, Konditor(in), Vater und Sohn, Dichter beim Open-Mic

Einleitung

Karriereorientiert sein heißt: umdenken[1]. Inwiefern muss man sich nach dem Studium (= nach der Uni) neu orientieren und was bedeutet „wie ein Profi auftreten[2]"?

Berufsorientiert denken und sich professionell ausdrücken sind Schlüsselfähigkeiten[3]. Ihre Kommunikation soll zielgerichtet[4] und teamorientiert sein. Denn es heißt: „Um zu den Profis zu gehören, muss man wie ein Profi denken." Wie man denkt geht Hand in Hand mit wie man spricht.

Vielleicht möchten Sie sich bei Kunden[5] besser ausdrücken[6] können. Vielleicht sind Sie der Kunde und Sie möchten Ihre Wünsche einem Verkäufer besser erklären können. Vielleicht wollen Sie Ihre Interessen mit anderen teilen. Vielleicht beantworten Sie Fragen bei einem Vorstellungsgespräch. Was braucht man dazu? Wie werden Sie Ihre Meinungen, Betrachtungen und Lebenserfahrungen klarer ausdrücken? Stellen Sie sich vor, Sie beantworten die Frage: Inwiefern muss man sich nach dem Studium neu orientieren und was gehört zu einem professionellen Auftritt?

Eine vielleicht nicht so gute Antwort wäre zum Beispiel:
Einfach besser reden und ein bisschen mehr über die Arbeitswelt sprechen.

Besser wäre ...

Aufgabe/Herausforderung

Während Sie die Vokabelübungen im Kapitel 1 durchnehmen, denken Sie daran, wie Sie obige Frage klarer und nuancierter beantworten können

Einstimmung auf das Thema

---

1 umdenken-think in a new way
2 wie ein Profi auftreten – present yourself like a professional
3 Schlüsselfähigkeiten-key skill areas
4 zielgerichtet-goal oriented
5 der Kunde, die Kundin-the customer
6 sich ausdrücken- express yourself

146

Was für ein Typ sind Sie?

schüchtern

extrovertiert

zurückhaltend

vorsichtig

ich bin meistens sehr positiv

aufgelegt

kontaktfreudig

Wie verhalten Sie sich am Arbeitsplatz?

ich trete sehr extrovertiert auf

ich spreche gern mit anderen, auch wenn ich sie nicht kenne

ich warte meistens, bis ich angesprochen werde

Geführter Dialog

Student(in) A	Student(in) B
Greet student B.	Return the greeting.
Ask the student if (s)he has worked in Germany.	Respond no, but you worked in Switzerland. It was two years ago. (vor zwei Jahren)
Ask if it was an internship (Praktikum) or a regular job (Dauerstelle).	Answer that it was an internship and that you learned a lot of German. Say that you also learned a lot about life at the workplace (am Arbeitsplatz)
Tell student B where you plan to work after college. (Ich habe vor, nach dem Studium bei _____ zu arbeiten.)	Tell student A that sounds good and good luck with it. (Das klingt gut; viel Glück dabei)

Now talk about jobs that you have had before and whether you liked the work or not. (Die Arbeit hat mir (nicht) gefallen.)

Also talk about friends and/or family and the jobs they have had.
Meine Eltern ...
Meine Geschwister ...
Mein Onkel, meine Tante ...
Mein bester Freund ...

Wie denken Sie?

innovativ   kreativ   realistisch   spontan   anders   berufsorientiert   zielorientiert

zielorientiert

außerhalb der Box

(mit neuen, quergedachten Ansätzen)

Am Thema dran bleiben!

Was gehört zum Thema unseres Kapitels? Streichen Sie alles durch, was <u>nicht</u> dazugehört.

1. Wir sind gekommen, um die Tische umzustellen.

2. Ich denke und spreche meist ganz spontan.

3. Ich spreche anders bei der Arbeit als bei mir zuhause mit Freunden.

4. Kein Mensch kann heute Vermögen aufbauen, ohne Aktien zu erwerben.

5. Man hinterlässt einen ersten Eindruck, sobald man das erste Wort ausgesprochen hat.

6. Das Siezen ist eher normal bei der Arbeit aber in Emails kann es anders: da schreibt man oft <u>ihr</u> und <u>euch</u>. (Wenn ich im Gespräch eine Person sieze, dann mache ich das auch in einer E-Mail genauso.)

7. Es gibt eine Einarbeitungszeit, bis man sein Arbeitsgebiet richtig beherrscht und als wertvoller Mitarbeiter betrachtet wird.

8. Einen Termin muss man einhalten.

Review

For the review section of this textbook, please skim the chapters again as needed, take note of challenging vocabulary words, and review all grammatical concepts. The pages that follow will guide you through the review process.

ACTIVE REVIEW

This section will help you clarify which topics you understand best and which topics require extra review.

Please Review each topic on the following pages by returning to that section of the textbook and taking brief notes. Topics are wherever possible listed in the order in which they appear in the textbook.

You may also supplement your knowledge by performing an internet search such as „verb conjugation German" and so on.

Introductions: Saying your name, where you come from, and where you live. Asking questions in basic introductions.

Verbs, verb infinites and verb stems. Conjugation endings.

The three genders and examples of nouns from each gender.

_____

_____

_____

_____

_____

_____

_____

_____

_____

_____

_____

_____

_____

_____

_____

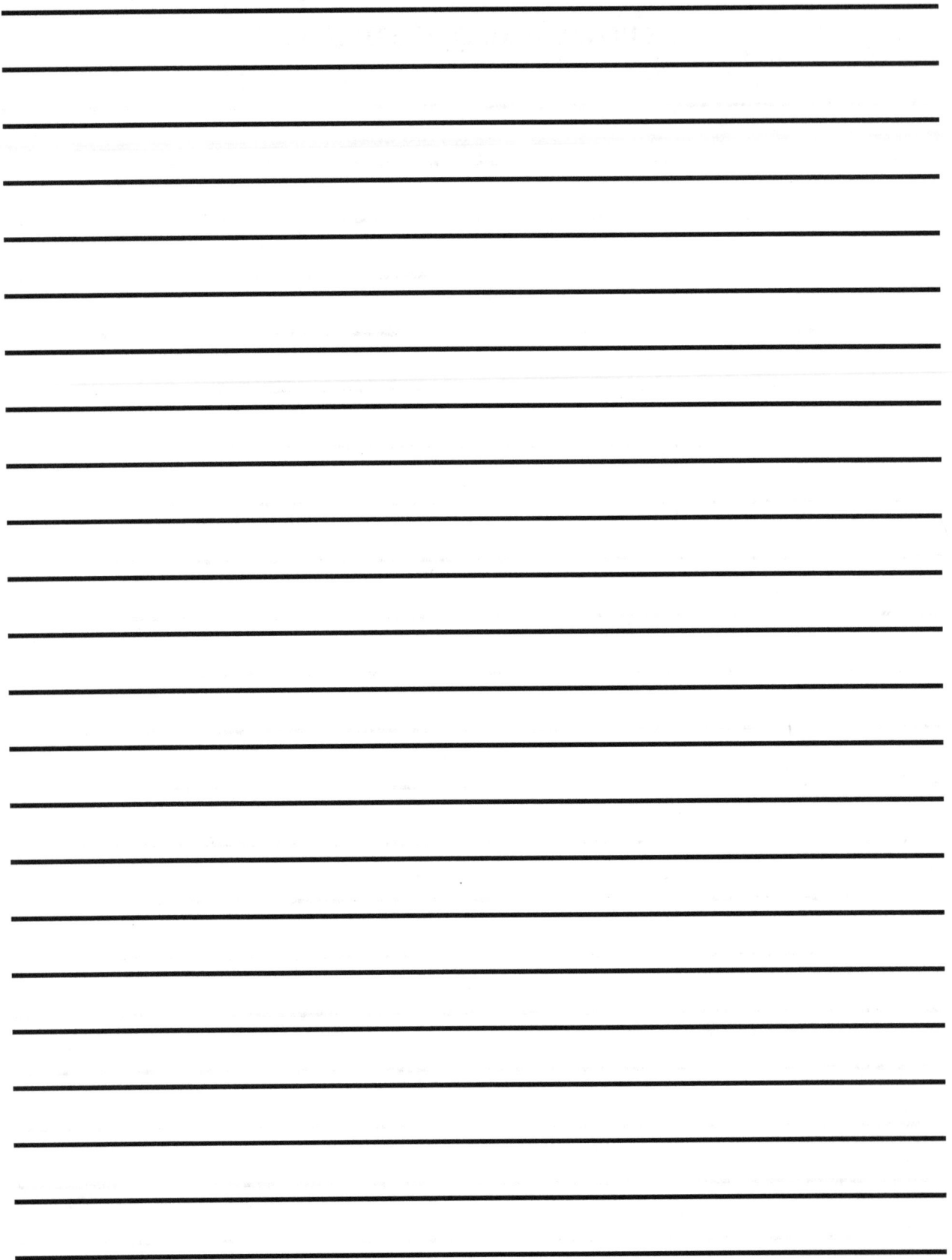

Formal versus Informal: Sie versus du and Wie geht es Ihnen versus Wie geht es dir?

_____

_____

_____

_____

_____

_____

_____

_____

_____

_____

_____

_____

_____

_____

_____

_____

mögen (ich mag) versus gern: when to use each expression and examples of gern.

_____

_____

_____

_____

_____

_____

_____

_____

_____

_____

_____

_____

_____

_____

_____

_____

Helping verbs in the present tense: Ich kann, Ich muss. How to combine them with a main verb and what they mean.

_____

_____

_____

_____

_____

_____

_____

_____

_____

_____

_____

_____

_____

_____

_____

_____

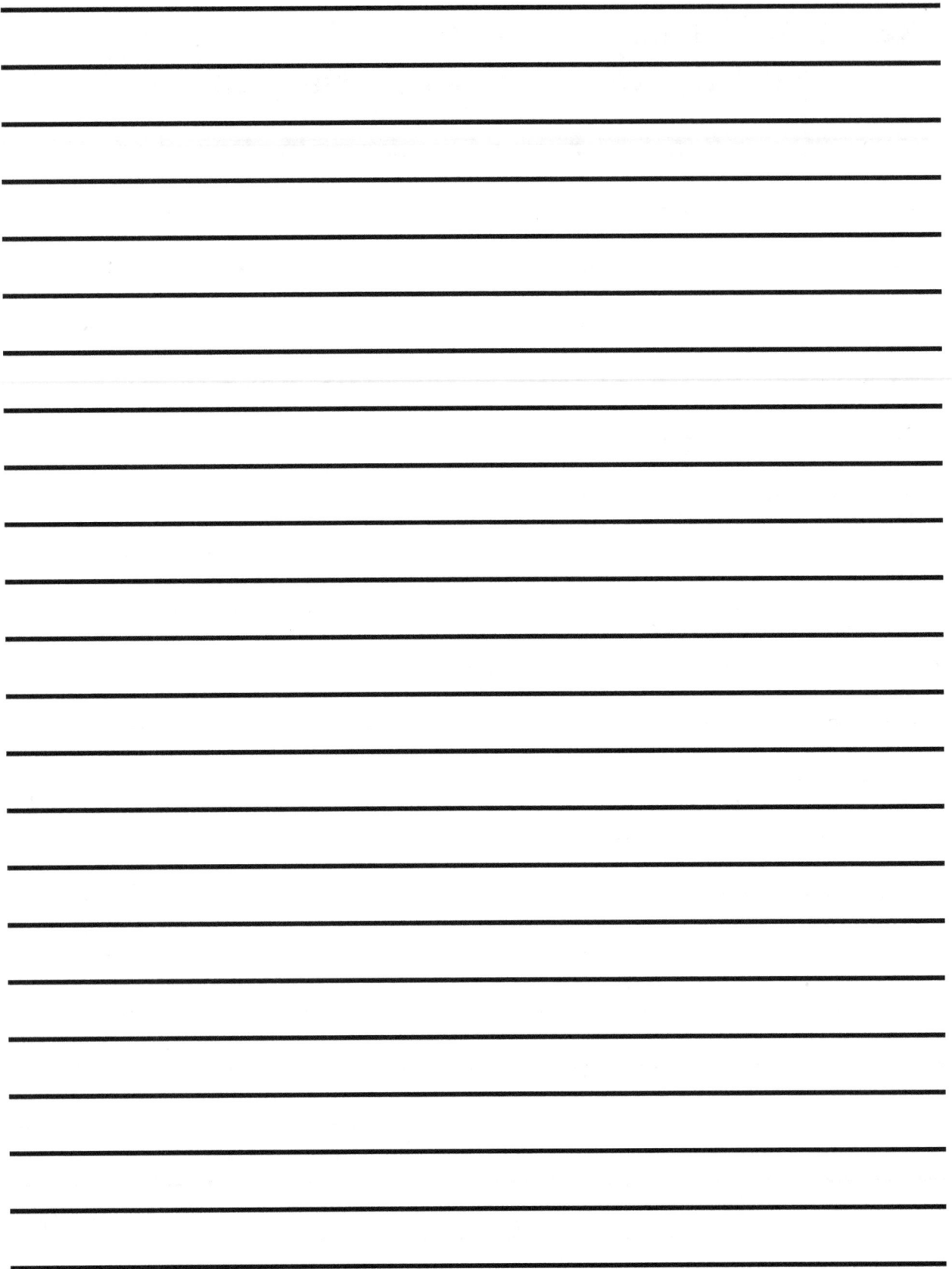

The future tense and the conjugation of werden.

Prepositions in German. Accusative Prepositions, Dative prepositions. Some examples of phrases using prepositions.

The four cases and the three genders (plus plural).

What is each case used for?	MASC	FEM	NEUT	PLUR
Nominative	der	die	das	die
Accusative				
Dative				
Genitive				

Numbers 1-20, days of the week, months.

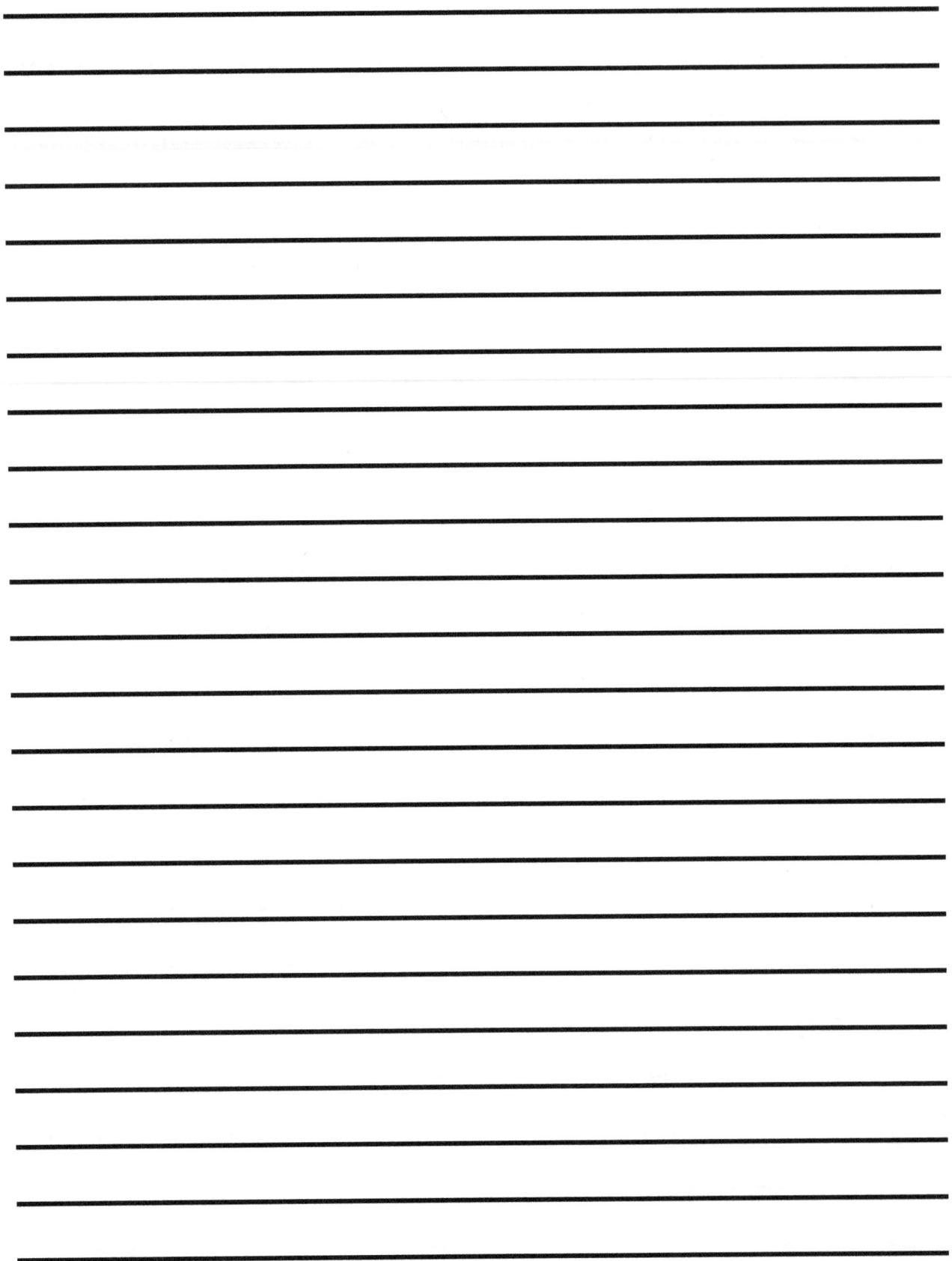

The Perfekt Tense using <u>haben</u> as a helping verb: examples and explanation.

_____

_____

_____

_____

_____

_____

_____

_____

_____

_____

_____

_____

_____

_____

_____

_____

_____

The Perfekt Tense using <u>sein</u> as a helping verb: examples and explanation.

_____

_____

_____

_____

_____

_____

_____

_____

_____

_____

_____

_____

_____

_____

_____

_____

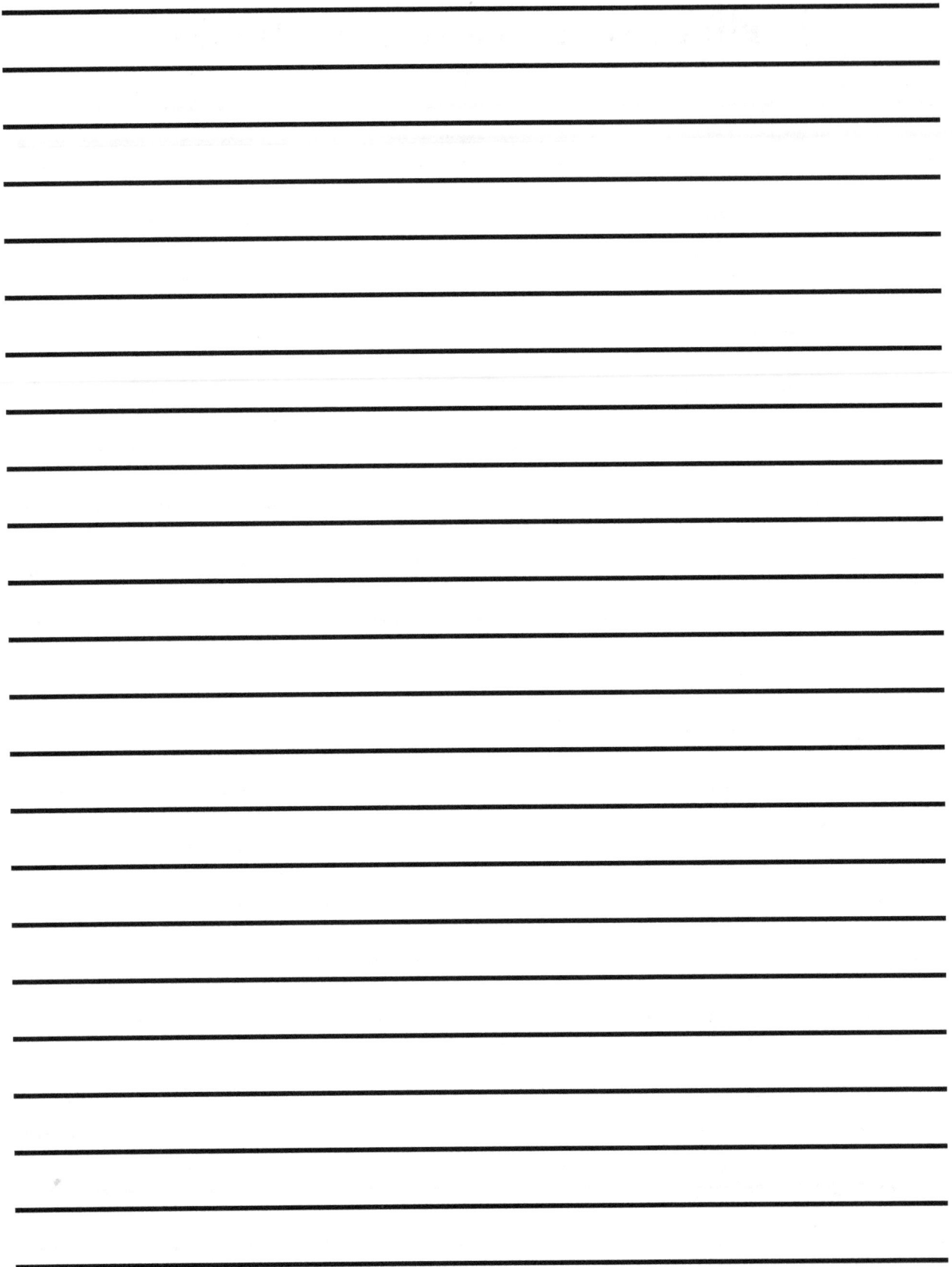

The Präteritum: another form of the past tense.

Separable Prefix Verbs

Reflexive Verbs

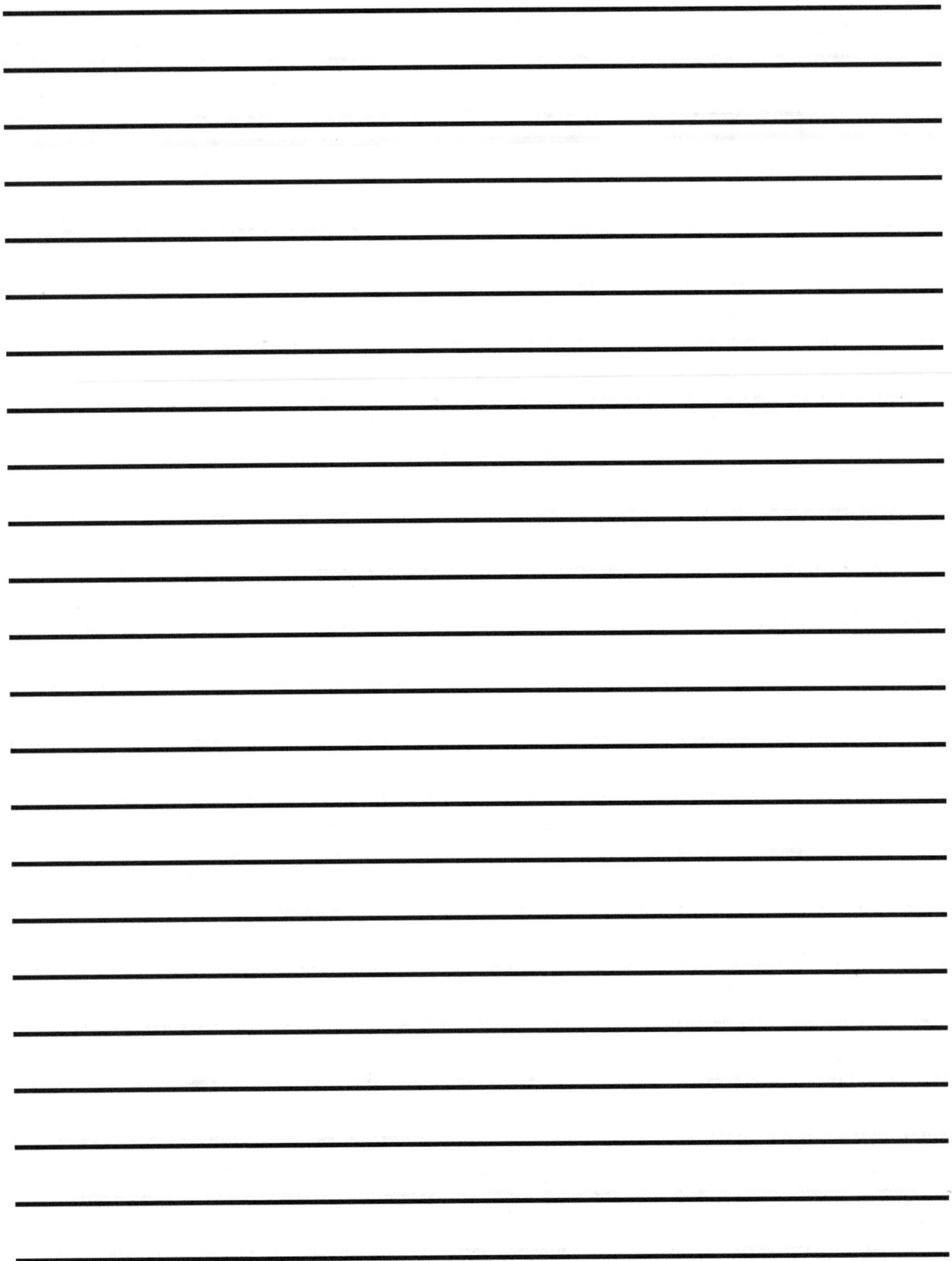

www.ingramcontent.com/pod-product-compliance
Lightning Source LLC
Chambersburg PA
CBHW081146040426
42445CB00015B/1784